California Condor
Flying Free

by Bonnie Graves

Perfection Learning®

Dedication

This book is dedicated to Tom and Emily Beecher—two talented California High School "California Condors"—now flying free!

And to the men and women whose efforts have helped return the California condor to its rightful place on the earth and in the sky.

About the Author

Bonnie Graves is the author of 12 books for young readers. Among these are *The Whooping Crane, The Best Worst Day,* and *No Copycats Allowed!*

Before Ms. Graves was an author, she was a teacher. Now she also writes books on teaching reading with her husband, Michael. They live on the edge of a huge park reserve in Bloomington, Minnesota, where they observe nature at their doorstep, ski, hike, bike, skate, and write their books.

Ms. Graves also likes to visit schools and encourage students to grow their own story ideas into books.

Cover Photo: CORBIS Royalty Free
Book Design: Deborah Lea Bell

Image Credits: **www.joelsartore.com** pp. 5(TOC), 6, 10, 22, 24, 25, 27, 28, 29, 32, 45, 51; CORBIS p. 7, 41

ArtToday(some images copyright www.arttoday.com) pp. 8, 9, 11, 13, 14, 15, 16, 17, 18, 20, 23, 31, 34, 37, 38, 42, 46-49, 52-53, 56-57; Corel pp.35, 39, 55, 58

Text © 2002 Perfection Learning® Corporation.
All rights reserved. No part of this book may be reproduced, stored in a retrieval system, or transmitted in any form or by means, electronic, mechanical, photocopying, recording, or otherwise, without prior permission of the publisher.

Perfection Learning® Corporation, 1000 North Second Avenue,
P.O. Box 500, Logan, Iowa 51546-0500.
Phone: 1-800-831-4190 • Fax: 1-800-543-2745
PB ISBN-10: 0-7891-5644-x ISBN-13: 978-0-7891-5644-0
RLB ISBN-10: 0-7569-0618-0 ISBN-13: 978-0-7569-0618-4
www.perfectionlearning.com
Printed in the U.S.A.

2 3 4 5 6 7 PP 13 12 11 10 09 08

Contents

1 Trouble at Matilija Creek 7

2 What Happened? 11

3 On the Wings of a Condor 19

4 Abandoned 24

5 Will It Live? 30

Epilogue: Capture 35

Recovery or Extinction? 42

California Condor Timeline 46

Flying Free 50

California Condor Facts 53

Glossary 58

Chapter

Trouble at Matilija Creek

Northwest of Ojai, California
February 1967

"Look, Mr. Connel!" Tim pointed downstream. A huge bird perched on a branch of a dead cottonwood tree.

"What is it?" Tim asked. "That's the biggest bird I've ever seen! It looks like a vulture."

"It's a young California condor. I'm sure of it," Mr. Connel answered. "Hurry and gather your fishing gear. We've got to call Dave."

"Why?" Tim asked.

"To let him know a condor's here," Mr. Connel replied. "Fewer than 100 California condors are left in the world. They're a very **endangered** species."

Mr. Connel and his son, Dave, knew all about birds. Dave was a **biologist**, working for the forest service.

"You mean they might become **extinct**? Like the dinosaurs?" Tim asked.

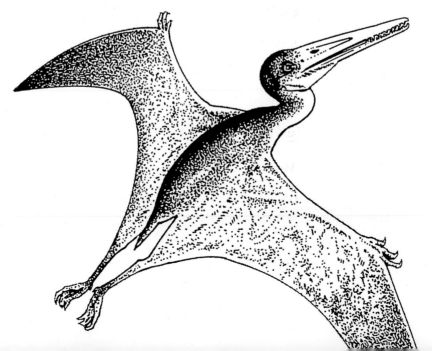

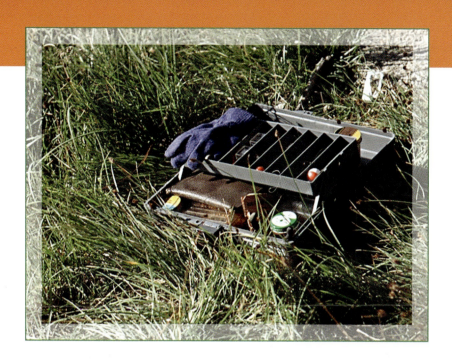

"That's right," Mr. Connel said, picking up his **tackle box**. "The condors haven't been able to replace themselves. And at the rate these birds are dying, the species could be extinct in another ten years. Once the last one's gone, there is no bringing the condors back."

Mr. Connel glanced at the condor. "And my guess is this one's in trouble."

"Why?" Tim wanted to know.

"It's too young to take care of itself," Mr. Connel answered. "I think it may have been **abandoned** by its parents."

"So it's an orphan," Tim said.

"Looks that way," Mr. Connel agreed. "And young condors can't survive on their own. Condors depend on their parents for a year or longer."

"Couldn't we leave it something to eat?" Tim looked in his lunch sack. All that was left was an apple. "My apple?"

Mr. Connel shook his head. "Afraid not. Condors are vultures. They eat **carrion**."

"Dead animals?" Tim made a face.

Mr. Connel nodded. "This condor may starve to death."

"Then we better hurry and call Dave," Tim said. "Before the bird dies!"

Chapter 2

What Happened?

"What happened to the California condors?" Tim asked as they walked quickly alongside the stream. "Why are there hardly any left?"

"Humans, Tim," Mr. Connel answered. "Fifteen thousand years ago, these birds flew over a large part of North America. Then the early settlers moved into condor country. That was the beginning of the end for the California condors.

"In the 1800s, condors flew from southwestern Canada to northwestern Mexico." Mr. Connel continued. "Then by the beginning of the 1900s, they could be found only in the **remote** mountain ranges of Southern California."

"So people shot the condors?" Tim asked.

"That's only part of it. They also poisoned and captured them. They collected the condors' eggs and reduced their food supply."

"The dead animals," Tim said.

Mr. Connel nodded. "Right. Like most other vultures, they don't kill their **prey**. They eat carrion."

"That's kind of gross!" Tim exclaimed.

"Well," Mr. Connel continued. "I suppose you could look at it that way. But people eat dead animals too."

"Yeah, but that's different," Tim chuckled.

"You bet it is," Mr. Connel said. "Condors help keep the earth clean by eating **carcasses**."

Mr. Connel picked up an empty soda can from the streambed. He frowned. "That's more than I can say for some humans!"

Mr. Connel continued. "Unfortunately, no animals have an appetite for the litter humans leave behind."

"So what sort of carrion do condors like to eat?" Tim asked.

"Well, long ago California condors ate carcasses of elk, deer, or beached sea animals," Mr. Connel replied. "That's before people arrived. When folks started settling the West, they destroyed wildlife **habitats**."

Tim looked up at Mr. Connel. "Why did they do that?"

"Well, they didn't do it on purpose, of course. The settlers cleared forests for farmland. They put up houses and buildings. What do you suppose that meant for the animals in the area?"

"They had to move out," Tim answered.

"Right. And what did that mean for the California condor?" Mr. Connel asked.

Tim replied, "No animals. No dead animals. No food."

"Right you are. The supply of animals shrunk. Today, the few condors that are left eat dead cattle, deer, and smaller animals."

Tim glanced down Matilija Creek. The young condor was still perched on the branch. Tim wondered if it was hungry. Was there any carrion around for it to eat? He didn't spot any. No dead animal bodies that he could see.

"So if there were enough dead animals around, would the condors be OK?" Tim asked.

"Not exactly," Mr. Connel answered. "Humans have caused other problems too. Power lines are a hazard. The birds fly into them. Another problem is poisoning by lead bullets."

"Lead bullets!" Tim exclaimed.

"Yes," Mr. Connel continued. "Condors eat them when feeding on **remains** that deer hunters leave behind.

"**Pesticides** in the environment are also a problem. They make the shells of the condors' eggs too thin. Condors have crushed their own eggs while sitting on them to hatch them.

"Human activity hasn't been kind to the California condor, Tim. It has taken away the three things condors need in their habitat. Can you guess what those are?"

The path back to the Jeep now jogged away from the stream. "Well, they need places to find food," Tim said. "That's one thing."

"Right," Mr. Connel nodded. "Available carrion. That's called *foraging habitat*. What else?"

"Hmmm," Tim thought as a big lizard and its baby skittered across the dirt path. "Well, they need to have babies, like you said. Otherwise, they'll die off. So I guess they need places to build their nests."

Mr. Connel smiled at Tim. "Right again. Their habitat needs to have places they can raise their young, like rock **crevices** or caves. And the third thing?"

Tim glanced around. He could no longer see the cottonwood snag where the orphaned condor perched.

"Dead trees to sit in!"

Mr. Connel laughed. "Right again. Condors need roosting sites, or places to rest in. Like cliff tops or trees."

Tim thought about the young condor in the tree. What would happen to it? Would it starve to death? Would Dave be able to do something? What about the rest of the condors? What if they died out like the dinosaurs?

Chapter 3

On the Wings of a Condor

It was a long hike back to the Jeep. Tim figured it would take them about half an hour. How long would the condor stay put?

"What will Dave do about the condor?" Tim asked.

"He'll call the forest service," Mr. Connel said. "Maybe they can think of something. Without parents, that bird doesn't have a chance on its own."

"Why?" Tim asked.

"Young condors don't know how to take care of themselves," Mr. Connel answered. "They're social creatures."

Mr. Connel went on. "Young condors learn by watching their parents and other condors. How long do you think *you* could survive in the wild on your own?"

Tim stopped in his tracks and looked around. There was nothing here to eat that he could see. Only **chaparral**, rocks, and scrub oaks.

How long could he live? He'd even been fishing for an hour and hadn't caught a thing. How *would* he get food on his own? He knew one thing for sure. He wouldn't find his favorite—pizza—lying around anywhere!

Maybe Tim would have to eat dead animals like condors did. Yuck! He couldn't imagine ever being *that* hungry!

"What if the condor flies away before the forest service gets here?" Tim asked.

Mr. Connel placed a hand on Tim's shoulder. "There's always that chance, Tim. But, my guess is, that condor doesn't have all its flight feathers yet.

"Also, the condor is not in a spot where it can easily take off and fly. If that cottonwood snag were on the side of a mountain instead of down in a **ravine**, I'd be more worried. All it takes are a few wing beats for an adult condor to be airborne."

"Wow!" Tim tried to imagine an adult condor taking off.

"How wide is a condor's wingspan?" Tim held both arms out, tackle box in one hand and rod in the other. "Six feet?"

"Nope," Mr. Connel answered. "Up to 9½ feet."

"No kidding!" Tim was surprised. "That's almost as wide as my bedroom."

Mr. Connel laughed. "They're the largest flying birds in North America.

If that condor had its flight feathers, it would circle higher and higher once it caught a warm air **updraft**. Then it would glide a long distance, seeking another updraft to take it even higher. Condors have been known to reach heights of 15,000 feet and speeds of more than 55 miles per hour."

"Wow!" Tim exclaimed.

Mr. Connel paused for a moment. "The southwestern Indians believe that their spirits are carried into the next world on the wings of a condor."

Tim stopped to catch his breath. The trail up the ravine was steep.

Tim looked up into the sky. He imagined a California condor soaring higher and higher into the clouds. He thought about the orphan condor in the tree. Would it get to soar one day? Tim hoped so. "We better hurry, Mr. Connel."

Chapter 4

Abandoned

At last, Tim and Mr. Connel reached their parking spot. "Why are you so sure the condor we saw was young, Mr. Connel? It sure looked big!"

"If it were an adult," Mr. Connel answered, "its head would be an orangish color. That condor's head was dark gray.

Not orange." Mr. Connel unlocked the Jeep and Tim hopped in.

"So why do you think the condor's parents left it?" Tim couldn't imagine his parents leaving him to take care of himself.

"That's a good question. And I don't know the answer." Mr. Connel started the motor. "California condors are generally good parents—even before the condor chick is hatched. Both Mom and Pop take turns sitting on the egg to keep it warm."

Slowly, Mr. Connel backed out of the parking area.

"You mean **incubating** it?" Tim asked.

"Right you are," Mr. Connel answered.

"How long does that take?" Tim had a lot of questions.

Mr. Connel put the Jeep in drive. "About 54 to 58 days."

"That's a little less than two months," Tim said.

"Yes, it is. About that time, the chick starts breaking out of its shell. It uses a hard, pointed knob on top of its beak. It's the egg tooth.

"The chick uses the tooth to make a tiny hole in the shell. That hole is called the *pip*. Then the chick turns in a circle inside the eggshell. As it turns, the egg tooth breaks through the shell."

"Sounds like a hard job for a little chick!" Tim exclaimed.

"Sometimes it is," Mr. Connel said.

"Sometimes a chick needs a little help from Mom and Pop."

"What do they do?" Tim asked.

"They tap on the shell to encourage the chick. The taps and sounds they make mean 'Hey, we're anxious to see you. Hurry up and come out!' "

Tim laughed. He had been anxious to see his little brother before he was born. That was before Tim knew what a pest his brother was going to be!

Mr. Connel continued. "After a chick hatches, both condor parents raise the chick. They take turns feeding it several times a day.

"The parents continue to bring the chick food until it's about six months old. That's about the time its feathers have come in. And that's when a condor takes its first flight.

"At about 10 or 11 months, a condor can fly well enough to follow its parents. Now they can lead their youngster to find food. They will also still feed it from time to time."

Tim looked out the window at the rolling hills. The recent rains had turned them green.

He imagined he could see two California condors soaring above the hills—the parents of the orphan condor! If only it were true. How great that would be! And what a sight!

Tim looked back in the direction of Matilija Creek. No condors to be seen. He just hoped the young condor wouldn't fly away before the forest service arrived.

Chapter 5

Will It Live?

"How long until we get to a telephone, Mr. Connel?" Tim asked.

"There's a service station about 15 miles from here. So I'd say about 15 minutes. You worried?"

"Yeah," Tim replied. "I don't want that condor to fly away and die. Not with hardly any California condors left in the whole world!"

"I'm with you, Tim," Mr. Connel agreed. "Even if it flies away, the forest service may still be able to find it."

"I hope so." Tim pointed to a dead deer on the side of the road. "Look!"

"Now, if that deer died in the wild, what do you suppose would happen to its body, Tim?"

"Condors would eat it."

"Maybe," Mr. Connel said. "Or some other **scavenger**. Scavengers are nature's garbage collectors—birds or animals that clean off carcasses. Otherwise the bodies rot or spoil."

"I guess nature thinks of everything," Tim said.

"See those books Dave left in the car?" Mr. Connel pointed to a stack of books at Tim's feet. "There's one on vultures. It has some pictures of condors. Take a look."

Tim found the book and the condor pictures. "Wow! These are cool!"

"See the head? How is it different from most other birds?" Mr. Connel asked.

"No feathers! It's bald," Tim said.

"Can you think of nature's reason for that?" Mr. Connel asked.

Tim thought for a minute. "Does it have to do with eating?"

"Yes," Mr. Connel answered.

Tim thought a minute. "OK. A condor tears at a carcass with its beak. Right? If it had feathers on its head, they'd get all bloody! Then how would the condor clean them?"

"Exactly," Mr. Connel said.

"Listen to this." Tim read from the book. " 'After eating, a condor will clean itself. It does this by wiping its head in sand or grass.' It would be a tough job getting a bunch of feathers clean!"

"What else does the book say?" Mr. Connel asked.

"It says condors have big appetites," Tim continued. "They eat enough at one feeding to last for two days or more!"

Tim had a big appetite too. Once he ate a whole pizza for dinner. But he was hungry again the next morning.

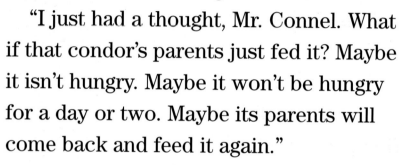

"I just had a thought, Mr. Connel. What if that condor's parents just fed it? Maybe it isn't hungry. Maybe it won't be hungry for a day or two. Maybe its parents will come back and feed it again."

"Maybe," said Mr. Connel hopefully. "Maybe."

Tim looked up from the book as they pulled into the gas station. Mr. Connel parked the Jeep. Tim walked with him to the telephone booth. Mr. Connel picked up the receiver and dialed.

"Hi, Dave," Mr. Connel said into the phone. "You'll never guess what Tim and I spotted down by Matilija Creek!"

Epilogue: Capture

The story you have just read is based on a true event.

A man named Mr. Connel really did spot a **fledgling** condor in the wild. He saw it one Saturday in February 1967, while he was fishing. He told Dave about it. Dave Connel was a U.S. Forest Service biologist.

So what happened next? More people were called. Dave Connel called John Borneman of the National Audubon Society.

The Audubon Society is a private organization that protects wildlife. Borneman then contacted Fred Sibley at the U.S. Fish & Wildlife Service.

The next day was Sunday. Sibley went to look for the condor. He didn't find it.

On Monday, three men went to find the condor. John Lorenzana, also a U.S. Forest Service biologist, Fred Sibley, and John Borneman went back to Matilija Creek. They hoped they could help the bird find its parents.

On their hike down to the creek, they met a woman. She had been getting water out of the creek.

"Did you see a condor down there?" they asked.

"So that's what that was!" the woman answered. "I thought it was a vulture. It's roosting in a cottonwood tree."

When the men reached the tree, they saw the bird perched on a branch.

They chased it off the cottonwood. They hoped it would fly *up* the canyon. That's where they thought its parents were.

Instead, the bird flew *down* the canyon. It landed in some chaparral on the steep slope of the canyon wall. Now the condor was perched about 100 feet above the creek. It was out of reach. What were the men going to do?

The three men returned to their offices. They called their bosses for advice. No one knew what should be done.

"Let's try to capture the bird," the men decided. "We'll take it to the Los Angeles Zoo."

The men knew people at the zoo who could check on the bird's health. These people would also work out a plan to get the bird back into the wild.

But the men knew they had to act quickly.

The next day was Tuesday. The three returned to the canyon. This time, they hoped to trap the bird with a net.

John Borneman climbed up the slope across from the condor. He kept an eye on the bird. The other two men carried a trout landing net about three feet in diameter. They climbed through the brush toward the bird.

Every once in a while, Sibley and Lorenzana poked their heads up through the brush. Borneman would point out the location of the condor.

At last, the men got close enough to net the bird. They tried, but failed. Again and again they tried. But each time, the bird flew farther down the canyon.

The men were tired and frustrated. But they were also determined. They could not let this bird go. The future of the species was at stake.

They would try again.

After taking a lunch break, Borneman changed places with Lorenzana. This time, Borneman and Sibley crawled through the brush and poison oak.

This time, the men didn't carry the net. They had another plan in mind.

Slowly, the men made their way through the brush. At last, they were close to where the fledgling condor perched.

Sibley sawed off a nearby 10-foot-long branch. They hoped to use the branch to catch the bird. They thought when it took off, they could use the branch to stop it. Instead, the young condor bounced off the branch and flew farther down the canyon!

By now, it was getting dark and cold. The three men were ready to give up. Then, just as they were about to leave, the condor flew into the air. It glided down to a strip of bare ground. The bird was exhausted, and so were the men. But they decided to make one last try.

The men sneaked up to the edge of the clearing. Sibley gave Borneman a roll of masking tape. Then the two men leaped through the brush toward the bird. Sibley grabbed the body. Borneman grabbed the head. He wrapped tape around the beak five or six times.

The condor immediately ripped the masking tape apart. It clamped its mouth on Borneman's hand, between his thumb and finger. It was then that Borneman found out what the inside of a condor's mouth was like!

The top of a condor's tongue is covered with rows of **barbs**. The roof of the upper jaw has barbs too. Borneman had to wait for the condor's mouth to relax before twisting his hand free.

The men then stuffed the bird into a duffel bag to protect its feathers. The three men made their way down through the thick brush to the dirt road where Borneman's vehicle was parked.

The men put the bird in a wire cage and fed it some raw hamburger. The condor gobbled that quickly!

"Well, we did it!" Borneman said. "Good job."

The men felt exhausted, but hopeful. Maybe now the bird had a chance.

The young condor spent the night in Borneman's garage. The next morning the men drove it to the L.A. Zoo. What would happen to the fledgling condor now?

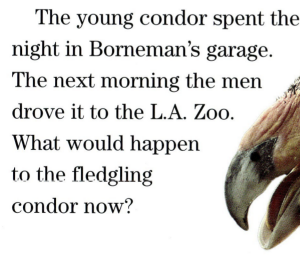

Recovery or Extinction?

The young condor spent the next ten days at the Los Angeles Zoo. It was named—TopaTopa.

TopaTopa was fed and cared for at the zoo. Then he (a guess, because both sexes look alike) was taken back to the place where he had been captured.

The hope was he could now make it on his own. For this to happen, TopaTopa would have to find food. He would need to keep out of harm's way.

For two more days, researchers watched TopaTopa through a telescope. He didn't eat. Other condors attacked him.

This condor would not make it in the wild. TopaTopa was taken back to the zoo.

That same year—1967—something important happened. The federal government made a list of endangered species. These species were given special protection.

The California condor was put on that list. With fewer than 100 of the species left in the world, it was in danger of dying out forever. What could be done?

The numbers of California condors had to be raised. That meant fewer birds had to die and more had to be hatched.

In 1975, the California Condor Recovery Team was established. The team was made up of people from five different groups—the National Audubon Society, the California Department of Fish and Game, the United States Forest Service, the United States Bureau of Land Management, and the United States Fish and Wildlife Service. Together these groups did many things to help the condor make a comeback. One of those things was to begin breeding the birds in **captivity**.

Breeding in captivity began in 1987. Just 27 California condors were left in the world. In 1988, the first captive-bred chick was hatched at the San Diego Wild Animal Park.

By the end of 1991, the condor population had risen to 53. In those three years, the population had increased by 25 birds.

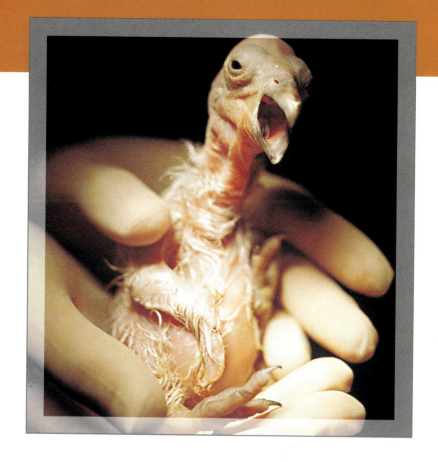

None of those chicks, however, was TopaTopa's. Biologists had learned by now that TopaTopa was indeed a male.

In 1993, TopaTopa finally became a father. His first offspring, Alishaw, was hatched. In that year, the population was up to 76. The California condor was making a comeback.

California Condor Timeline

This timeline will help you track the California condor's recovery.

Population	Date	What happened
About 60	1967	Topa Topa captured and kept in L.A. Zoo. Condor placed on federal endangered species list.
Unknown	1971	California condor placed on California endangered species list.
Unknown	1975	California Condor Recovery Team established. A recovery plan adopted.
Unknown	1976	Critical habitat established in nine Southern California areas.

Unknown	1980	California Condor Research Center established.
27	1981	California Department of Fish and Game (CDFG) permits breeding in captivity.
24	1982	L.A. Zoo builds condorminiums—flight cages for condors.
27	1985	Decision made to capture all free-flying California condors.
27	1986	Chumash Indians express concern about capturing the condors. They view these birds as sacred.
27	1987	Last of the free-flying condors, AC-9, captured. Breeding in captivity begins.

Population	Date	What happened
27	1988	First chick, Molloko, bred in captivity hatched in San Diego Wild Animal Park!
28	1989	Four more chicks hatched in Los Angeles and San Diego.
32	1990	Eight chicks hatched in captivity.
40	1991	Began releasing condors back into the wild. Thirteen chicks hatched.
64	July 1992	First condor bred in captivity is released.
76	July 1993	On April 27, TopaTopa's first offspring, Alishaw, is hatched!
89	July 1994	Sixteen chicks hatched in captivity. One dies.

Population	Date	What happened
104	July 1995	Seventeen chicks hatched in captivity. Two die.
121	July 1996	Eighteen chicks hatched in captivity.
134	July 1997	
153	July 1998	
162	July 1999	Eighteen chicks hatched.
169	July 2000	
162	Jan. 1 2001	

Note: As of April 1, 2001, condors had laid 35 (34 captive and 1 wild) eggs. Four of those had hatched.

Flying Free

Today, there are about 170 California condors in the wild and in captivity. Of those 170 birds, about 50 are flying free. All these free-flying birds were bred and raised in captivity.

Before condors can be released, they need to learn to behave like condors. The training begins right after they are hatched. In order to survive on their own, condors have to know how to find food and water. They also need to know how to find roosting and nesting sites.

Until 1982, TopaTopa was the only condor in captivity. Today, there are about 120 keeping him company at the Los Angeles Zoo.

Captive condors live in condorminiums. These homes are about twice the size of a basketball court. They have a mesh ceiling about 22 feet high. There is enough room for the condors to fly. The birds also have water pools and places to roost and nest.

Three different places have condorminiums. These are the Los Angeles Zoo, San Diego Wild Animal Park, and the World Center for Birds of Prey in Boise, Idaho.

Condors soon to be released live in field pens. These enclosures are near the area where the condors will be released. In December 2000, thirteen condors were waiting in pens to be released.

Condors have been released in three places—Arizona, Central California, and Southern California. How long has it taken for 50 condors to fly free again?

About 20 years!

It has taken 20 years to raise the condor population from a low of under 25 to around 170 birds today.

Because of the efforts of many people, the California condor is making a comeback—slowly, but surely.

However, the species is not out of danger. But if we are lucky and careful, the California condor may once again take its rightful place in the earth's **ecosystem**. And you, one day, might be able to see this magnificent bird high above you, flying free.

California Condor Facts

Height: about 3½ to 4½ feet tall

Weight: 17 to 24 pounds

Wingspan: 9½ feet

Color: Condors have bare heads that vary from pink to orange, with shadings of yellow, red, and light blue. Around their necks are **ruffs** of black feathers. The body feathers are completely black, except for the triangles of white on the underside of the wings. These can be seen only when the condors spread their wings.

Features: Condors have bare heads and necks. This makes it easier for the condors to keep themselves clean while eating carrion. Condors have no vocal chords. They communicate through body language, grunts, growls, and hisses.

Family Life: California condors usually pair for life at about 5 to 7 years of age. Condor males perform a courtship dance in front of the females. After several weeks of spending time together, they mate. Sometime between mid-January and mid-April, each female lays a single egg. Condor parents take turns sitting on the egg to hatch it. The sitting condors rotate the egg many times a day. Each condor pair usually produces only one egg every two years.

Habitat & Home: Condors live in places with little human activity. Condors need a habitat where they can find nesting and roosting sites and plenty of food. Condors build their nests in rock crevices, caves, or hollows of very large trees. The females lay their eggs in shallow holes. These nests are called *scrapes* because condors scrape them out with their feet and beaks.

Andean condor

Food: carrion

Social Life: Condors are social animals. They flock together for many daily activities, such as flying, finding food, and eating. They also have a **pecking order**. A condor that is high in the pecking order gets the best spots to hunt and the most to eat.

Enemies & Survival: California condors' main enemy is a lack of habitat because of human activity and ignorance.

Life Span: Condors live 50 years or more.

Where Found: Condors are found in **isolated** areas of California and Arizona

Population: In January 2001, there were a total of 162 California condors in the wild and captivity.

Cousins: California condors are part of a group called New World vultures. There are seven species of New World vultures. Among these are the Andean condor (wingspan is 10 feet) and the turkey vulture (most common of the species).

Turkey vulture

Glossary

abandoned — left behind with no support

barb — sharp point

biologist — person who studies plants and animals

captivity — state of being held in a protected place

carcass — dead body

carrion — meat of a dead animal

chaparral — thicket of small evergreen oaks

crevice — narrow opening in a rock wall

ecosystem	community of plants and animals
endangered	nearly extinct (see separate glossary entry)
extinct	gone forever; no longer living
fledgling	bird that has not learned to fly and cannot take care of itself
habitat	place in the environment where an animal normally and naturally lives and grows

incubate	to sit on eggs until they hatch
isolated	away from the population
pecking order	pattern of social organization
pesticide	chemical used to control insects on crops
prey	animal taken by another for food
ravine	small, narrow, steep-sided valley
remains	dead animals
remote	out-of-the-way; secluded

ruff feathers around the neck of a bird

scavenger animal that feeds on carrion (see separate glossary entry)

tackle box container with compartments to hold fishing supplies, such as hooks, sinkers, lures, and so on

updraft upward movement of air

Acknowledgements

This book would not have been possible without the assistance and expertise of a number of individuals. First of all, I am deeply indebted to John Borneman of the National Audubon Society, one of the three men who helped capture the fledging condor TopaTopa, for giving me a detailed description of TopaTopa's capture and for reading the manuscript for accuracy. I also want to thank Dr. Michael Wallace, Los Angeles Zoo's Curator of Conservation and Science and the California Condor Recovery Team Leader, who helped me with my initial research and gave me an "up close and personal" tour of the Los Angeles Zoo's condorminiums where I was able to view these extraordinary birds firsthand; Katherine Gould, former Webmaster of the Los Angeles Zoo, who so graciously supplied me with research material; and Ron Jurek, Wildlife Biologist, Habitat Conservation Planning Branch, California Department of Fish and Game, who aided me in my quest for firsthand source material and supplied me with up-to-date population counts.

Special thanks are also due to Jerry Brunetti who alerted me to the California condor's plight and planted the idea for this project, and to editors Sue Thies and Judy Bates who helped it grow into a book.

For More Information
Web Sites
www.lazoo.org
www.peregrinefund.org/notes_condor.html
www.dfg.ca.gov/kids/t&e4kids/condor.html
http://endangered.fws.gov/i/b0g.html
www.sandiegozoo.com/special/condor/home.html